Haile Tesfaye was born and raised in Sudan. He spent most of his early childhood being a shepherd and providing the necessities for his family. He migrated to New Zealand with his family in 2002, and has since acquired a university degree, along with other courses, to become an expert in the field of podiatry. Surviving a war-torn existence has taught him to create a path for hope in the face of suffering.

The splinter in the mind

Haile Tesfaye

The splinter in the mind
© Haile Tesfaye 2017

All rights reserved. No part of this publication may be reproduced, stored in a retrieval system, or transmitted in any form or by any means, electronic, mechanical, photocopying, recording or otherwise, without the prior written permission of the author.

National Library of Australia Cataloguing-in-Publication entry

Creator: Tesfaye, Haile, author.

Title: The splinter in the mind/Haile Tesfaye.

ISBN: 9780648139706 (paperback).

Subjects: Poetry.

Published with the assistance of www.wordwrightediting.com.au

All images courtesy of www.pexels.com with the exception of *Mustard seeds* on page 34, courtesy of Sanjay Acharya (permission under GNU Free Documentation Licence, details available at: https://commons.wikimedia.org/wiki/File:Black-mustard-seeds.jpg).

Acknowledgements

First and foremost, I wish to express my deep and sincere gratitude to my parents for their sacrifices so that I may have a good life. They have been the central inspiration and motivation to yearn for knowledge and be a master of life — I therefore dedicate this book to them. Speaking of encouragement, I appreciate all the support I have received from my siblings and friends. And finally, many thanks to the New Zealand government for opening the door to an exile from a war-torn country, allowing me to migrate and become a permanent resident, and experience a different side of the world.

The splinter in the mind

A conscious and curious universe,
a product of vibrant flux and vortex
sprung into one colossal maelstrom.
The root is a dilemma that has driven
mankind mad, like a plank in the eye and a
splinter in the mind. Nothing is coincidence,
for all things need uncaused infinite force to
bring substances into existence, and to
assert that a lesser life begets an intelligent
being is a paradox that defies reason.

A kiss of betrayal

The knives of a foe are heavy to bear, but the kiss of betrayal from those you hold dear shatters the heart in two. And when faith escapes like sand through the fingers, solitude takes hold.

Prey to existence

To be conscious is to be prey, like a mouse to an owl. Therefore, sow wherever there is hope, before the heart is tangled in thorns and is crushed by the rock that dries its oil up.

No greater love

No greater gift is bestowed than the love that giveth freely and moves thy neighbour's mountain concealed in mist.

Be the pilot of your life

The world is like a carnival mirror that distorts thoughts and conceals things that are out of order. Therefore, do not let pride clothed without humility guide you, but be the pilot of life so that you may sail through the thunderstorm and not drift into the dark water.

Haile Tesfaye

The fall of the flock

Take heed of thyself, for wicked
shepherds have deceived the
flock from the fountain of living
water. The world has come to
be a place of thorns and thistles
in which suffering and death
abound, striking down like
a sword.

The silent God

Life taunts man like
an oasis, but it is in
darkness that light is exposed. Therefor great
love speaks to us in utter silence and suffering.
And behold the glory
of his essence still hovers in
the air in His absence.

Smell of death

A wicked mind with a dismal heart of evil deeds. Even animals scatter away when man is around, as they can see the rage in his eyes and smell death emanating from his pores.

The flame of a refiner's fire

The truth is, the flame of a refiner's fire purges the impurities out of life and leaves the spirit and flesh intact. But that of an incinerator will consume and destroy extensively.

Painted rose

If a rose is vibrant and has a pleasant smell, would the colour matter? Then why do we cast some aside and give hell to our own kind? Is it not sufficient that we fail in our own mind?
There is no greater sin than to loathe and value a life less based on one's belief or race.

The language of God

Fortitude does not grow
on trees, and there is no greater weapon
than silence for it giveth peace. It douses
the flames of anxiety
and tortures those who
seek revenge, while it
spawns meekness in the
hothead.

The anxiety of life

Be on guard or the anxiety
of life will embed shards
deep within the heart, and
peel the layers off to pour
salt on raw wounds.

War is a piteous roar

What is war but a piteous roar?
It is a miserable
obsession of terror
that bribes the bearer
to rend blades for
dogma and bigotry.

The filter of life

The Nazarene is the salt that
preserves the good in man and
excludes the rotten influence. He
is the filter that guides the world
through the perilous waters of
life.

Surrender to divine providence

The world will not provide contentment for the dreary and empty lives of mankind, but greater pleasure and fulfillment is found in the spirit that gave him the breath of life.

Mind over matter

Do not mind the things that do not matter, nor despise the world, but pick up a stone and hurl it at the oppressor.

Comrades of life

That which cometh from the dust of the ground is fragile yet taketh superior position. A weapon will not vanquish, for a fruitful tree with a strong root will not suffer the axe.

The measure of greatness

A cruise ship will reroute its path to avoid the storm in order to reach its destination. Likewise, the resistance you conquer during the journey to obtain your purpose is the real measure of greatness.

The essence of salt

The essence of salt is its flavour, similarly the conscience is the soul of man. Death is the end of consciousness for the sheep, but for the goat it's the beginning of eternal crisis.

The man in the mirror

The judgment of the world will pass, what the man in the mirror has to say counts. When all is said and done, the verdict that matters the most is the reflection that stares back from the glass.

Heart of men

It is a feeble spirit, and black,
in the human heart that lures
men to wicked ways.

One God, many faces

The mind is constructed
with multiple windows, and each
being elects which one to peer through onto
the world, but the truth is distinguished
by its path, not grace, therefore it is a
paradox that defies reason to believe
that there is one God with many
faces.

The tree of life

The tree of life links mankind
in roots of genes. It began as a
seed sown, and grew into branches
rich with offspring of every kind, but
the bitterness of the world has trembled
its core, causing some leaves to fall and
vanish in the void, while others ponder on
fate and wonder on the origin of their traits.

The smog that fills the skies

Mortal sins with tainted lies. Your desire is to possess, not appreciate. Man in struggle in the grip of love, like oil and water, incapable of uniting to be one element. Our destructive entity has kept us estranged, and the human race is the smog that fills the skies.

The truth is in the belief

Faith is felt in the mind, love is found inside the heart, but the truth is in the belief.

Wells of the world

The wells of the world are empty and dry, but in Christ alone there is living water, with an eternal supply that will fill the heart and soul with abundant joy.

The rib cage of a man

The finest portion of a man was fashioned from the bone that protects the centre of his existence, his heart, and his lungs that bear the breath of life. A woman was made to complete the man, just as the rib cage supports the body.

Black in the human heart

There is a black hole in the human heart which even the universe cannot contain, but a love vast and eternal can.

The missing link

Judaism and Christianity are
nothing but a mirror image of
each other, for one cannot be
fulfilled without the other. One
continues to anticipate the Messiah,
while the other has recognised him.

The grand deception

The eye is the doorway to the soul.
That which appears pleasurable to the eye
can poison the heart.
Therefore, recognise the elements,
for appearances are deceiving, just as what is sour can
seem pleasant. And so what good is a man
with a core filled with corpse rot?

A reminder of who we are

A mirror reminds
a man of his inner
condition when
he forgets.

When a life enters the world

An infant enters the world
like a lit candle that is warm
and soothing, even the sun is
insignificant, for the newborn's
light shades its magnificence.
But when the darkness perceives
the flame that is burning, it will
turn the wax to fumes.

Time and life

Time is lighter than a feather,
and man was created within to
be greater, yet it is so powerful
beyond measure that it slips
through his fingers.

When death knocks

When death knocks on the door,
I question the destiny of humanity.
I wonder, after our last breath, will
we finally find rest from all this
pain and oppression?

The heart is the candle

The heart is the candle.
When it is not guarded,
the wolves will blow it
out, and when it dims,
light fades and it
becomes empty, like a
room covered in
darkness.

Trapped like a fly under glass

Man has been trapped, like a fly under a glass, to a mindset where he must do and obey what society says, but those rules do not apply, as the war we blindly fight is imposed by fear. If this order remains in power, humanity will lose its emotions, and only know what it sees and believe what it's been told.

Circle of life

Life begets death, and when a seed leaps from the soil and blossoms, another withers.

Flawless faith

Faith is wisdom and courage that
giveth power to defy logic. Consider
the little birds, even though the gust
makes their legs tremble, their flawless faith
helps spread their wings to fly. Learn from the little lilies,
for their belief guards them from spinning, and
empowers them to grow straight.

When the soil ceases to support

The wise and meek are
the root and impetus of
society, but one day the
soil will cease to support,
and all that is on top will
collapse and get swallowed
into the ground.

Lost star

At dawn the stars
shone with glory,
but of a sudden,
one vanished and
the chain of light
was broken. The
search since then
has been unceasing,
and the world has
lost its joy.

Power of prayer

There is no trial or weapon
that is known on earth that
can defeat what the power of
prayer can do alone.

The parent of knowledge

Faith possesses elements of doubt, yet it's beyond the boundaries of knowledge, as one is a choice and the other is an understanding. Similarly, knowledge may discover the beginning of the universe, but the origin of being itself is a fertile field for faith, as to comprehend the uncaused cause is a paradox that defies reason.

Duo of heartbeats

A heart has two characters, one is young, the other is old.
And when one weeps, the other forbears,
and this duo hath yielded wines of
sin that it cannot guard.

Becoming one

Marriage is two becoming one. It's a communion with a constant compromise, and to share a life one ought to sacrifice autonomy. But the gain is well worth the loss.

Four parts that make a day

Mornings hold hope, afternoons aim to fulfil that goal, and evenings carry the memories of the entire day, but night is where peace is present.

Who is Jesus?

Born of a virgin,
begotten as a
man, but he has
always existed as one
God who manifests
himself as three co-equal
and co-eternal persons.

Overcome adversity

Take misfortune as a lesson.
Learn to find rest from oppression.
Expect to be punished when asking,
but never give in, keep your essence and
be grateful for all of the blessings.
Take action and turn adversity into
ambition.

The moral nature of man

The shining morning star, created with a moral compass, but possessed by desire. A change of inner nature begot chaos and abandoned its offspring with stray thoughts. Seek from within and you'll truly find what is sought. And behold, leave the world behind and willingly sail across the windy sea and shores to discover the absolute moral codes.

The anchors of life

Gravity anchors the mind, fear kills the soul, and love silences the world but defends the heart.

A wicked generation

Men of this era
are both hungry
wolves and
slaughtered
lambs.

Tomorrow

Yesterday's burden is but today's lesson and tomorrow is just a dream of hope. Therefore, let not your spirit be anxious by what's been done and by a day that does not yet exist. Consider the creatures that soar through the sky and creep upon the earth, they do not let the resentment of days gone by and the fear of what's to come drive them insane, for they know to live one day at a time.

Faith of a mustard seed

The faith that is planted with a mustard seed will not wither, even if the dust of doubts sows over the soil. But be careful, for insects and rodents will scrabble their way into the garden of the heart.

Wake up, humanity

Nature is struggling and humanity is dying. We're fading like the leaves on moist earth lying. We have tongues of forgiveness, but minds of ignorance. There is a reason for our existence, but from segregation we must distance, since what we create seems to lead us to our own extinction.

The power of unity

When love and peace unite, man will cease to fight.

Hope for future generations

The world is a battle zone.
To survive, knowledge is the
only weapon. And education
is the hope the future
generation needs to cope.

Cup of suffering

When the way is dim and bleak, be glad
and drink from the cup of suffering so that
ye may wear the crown of peace.

The elements of evil

Evil is like a molecule. It's caused by multiple elements, of which fear is the root, lust is the branch and pain is the leaves. Though violence is sometimes necessary to dismiss evil, the only antidote is love.

Root of self-war

Fear activates war. When it knocks, send courage to open the door.

The power is in the people

Fear not and address the issue. The power is in the people, never let politicians possess your rights and oppress you.

The entirety of God

Man and woman are both extensions of God. Man represent God's image, whereas woman symbolises his emotions. But when both come together, they characterise the entirety of God.

Origin of life

Life is a product of nothingness, but
is not buffeted by random choice.
Out of the void a burst of light existed.
A cosmos was awakened to the death
of darkness with authority, and it will
cause catastrophe to those not
abiding by its rules.

The beginning of the end

Do not believe
those that say
peace is on its
way, as the worst
trial and tribulation
are yet to come.

A cosmic battle

Through design the universe exists the way it is.
And life is a cosmic battle between the righteous and
the wicked.

The truth will prevail

That which will expose the
treacherous is the gaze of the
multitude and a knowledge of
himself. Therefore, do not
condemn the guilty when accused falsely,
for all deceits concealed from
the truth in the dark will be
revealed in the light.

The covenant of the rainbow

A thunder awakens the soul to ravage. Lightening frightens the mind. Destructive wind tears the heart apart. But a rainbow never fails to bring a smile as it shines its colourful lights to fade the frown the rain bought down. And so when the darkness invades and nothing in life makes sense, stare towards the sky, for just as the sun peeks through the thunderous clouds, so will hope to end the storm.

The oyster

When a grain of sand
enters the oyster's shell,
a vexing pain exists. The
oyster complains not, but
accepts the agony and allows
the misery to create a path
for joy to flow. Remember, the
things that get under your
skin and the many trials
of life will become a comely
pearl through patience.

Commodity of the rich

Poverty is a curse created by man.
It's employed by the powerful and rich as a
good commodity so that the poor and meek
may fade.

A path to follow

Shadow Christ,
not Christians.

Rise from the dead

Consider the flowers that flourish, and
yeast that rises when its baked.
Learn from the trees, from seeds,
they rise to great heights. Be like
the ocean, for the tide at times falls, but in
the end it will always rise. Take a lesson
from the sun, even though it sets every night,
daily it does rise. Believe as ye will,
rise and transform from a lamb unto
a lion.

A war zone

A world without rules
has no equality, and
without mercy, justice
is an animal that knows
not what it does. Therefore, the
world is a war zone, you
need to be a soldier.

The wheel of fortune

Fate is a return
of what you gave.
It will either hold
a delightful destiny
or return to tear
your world apart.

The stepping stone

Infirmity is the stepping stone
to conquer adversity, and rejection is the
highest form of acceptance.

Misconception of evolution

Evolution has no authority
to enlighten how things came
in to being, but it can certainly
display the vicissitudes life
had to adapt to over time to
survive. Therefore, when
science pledges to behave
as though it has the answers to
all questions, it slays itself.

The bird in the cage

An invisible prison, like a bird in a narrow cage that is able to see a small shaft of light and freedom in the distance, but is unable to venture out through the open gate and leap on the back of the wind and soar through the sky. When humanity refutes the notion that life exists only through a dust-covered window, then ye will comprehend thou has the key and no longer live in a self-imposed prison.

The battlefield

In the war between good and evil,
the heart is the battlefield, while
the mind is the weapon. A tyrant
will die multiple times
before his death, but
a valiant man dies only
once.

The dawn of a better world

When will it be, the day when
preachers of hate will be silenced
and nation will not lift weapons
against nation, but man will live
in harmony and become his
brother's keeper?

Rules of life

Trust none except
the true one God.
Listen to your heart,
follow yours dreams,
believe in yourself,
have faith in others.
Settle for nothing,
always do your best,
know what you're capable of.
Expect people to doubt you,
use that as motivation.
Challenge everything,
fight for what you believe,
let nothing back you down.
Not all will love you, but do
good to them anyway.
Appreciate all criticism,
learn something new,
take on every opportunity,
forget all the unnecessary.
Remember where you started,
push beyond any limits,
bend all the rules.
Take mighty risks,
live on the edge, yet stay safe.
Seize every moment.
Life is truly a gift so
live it to its fullest.

The rib that protects

In humility a woman shows
a man the power of emotion,
and in her gentle calmness,
she displays her strength, but
in her love, she expresses and
reminds man that she's the rib
that protects his inner self.

Where the struggle began

All of life's struggle began
in the dark, inside a woman's
womb, and we remain
troubled until we return back
to the tomb.

Fading flower

The world is like a
fading flower, lost
in the current of the
dark raging sea of
sin.

The roses of today

The youth of today
are born like roses
with perfect colours.
But as they journey
through life, they
become the petals
that wither with thorns
who never receive the
time to grieve until
they're gone.

Wine of love and lust

Love thrives on patience,
but lust on temptation.
One is the ecstasy that
carries temporary satisfaction,
but the other is a divine grace
that brings fulfilment.

Eternal paintbrush

The cosmos and all life
forms are not a product
of arbitrary chance, but
all are branches created
out of glory through an
eternal paintbrush.

Power of the pen

The tongue can practise what it preaches,
but what has been proved is that, to the farthest
corner and inner universe, words can reach.
The pen is mightier than any double-sided
sword. Through ink and written words,
the world was changed.

As lonely as the Earth

The creator and creation
planned to be held in
eternal bond. Yet we are
as solitary as the earth is
in the galaxy. Is humanity forever
separated from a God that
may well have existed before time?

Created hungry

A gardener starving for knowledge; as he began
to indulge his desire, the body's lamp opened its eyes
and released a dim light into his soul. This was the birth
of all exiles and wandering.
The axe lies at the root of our foundation.
We are one out of many branches of a mourning tree.

Pay in kind

Befriend your foes,
and do good, not woes.
Give others their due,
and pay in kind, for what
you do and say will come
back to haunt you. Blessed
are those who give back
more than what they got
and in return expect nothing.

The power of a smile

A smile gives
life and fondles
the soul in bliss.

Violence

Violence in quest for justice is virtuous, but in pursuit of vengeance, it's wicked.

An insecure God

A mortal shell longing to be recognised, utterly alone in the cosmos, floating like a tiny rock. Blindly obedient, like the wolves that howl at the moon, also is man to an insecure God. A king who sits at his throne only to stare down with a heart of stone, who adores the power to bend one's will like a twig.

The axis of evil

Rotten fruits bear corrupt labour.
A nation built on political purpose
will flourish on violence, so
men are not terrorists, but it's their
doctrine that impels them to commit
all kind of immoral and wicked acts.

The plague and the cure

Faith is the medicine that cures the soul.
Religion is a plague that spreads
to multiply. It is the drug
that fails to feed
the poor, but starts
all the wars.

A soulmate

A soulmate is like a mirror in which one sees a reflection of oneself.

The universal quest

Existence is like a maze, it has multiple directions, but only one way. If life is only just a spark in the candle of the sun, then death is but an insignificant accident. We are energy that never disappears, but transfers into the next room.

The caterpillar's journey

All life form begins inside a shell. The caterpillar has a restricted existence, although its insight and perspective are limited, it understands its potential. It struggles to be free, but regardless of the obstacles, it continues to crawl and grow till it bursts through the skin to take a new form as a butterfly, leaving the old behind.
The colours of the butterfly represent transformation and resurrection. Man must understand and learn to trust the journey and process of growth, for the possibilities of what we can become are endless.

Stitched into emptiness

A generation with hollow smile, in terror with no hope of escaping despair. But nothing exists without a purpose, and he that walketh in the path he knoweth will not vanish. Men sceptical of faith will be stitched into emptiness, and he that abandons reason will have no root for decision, but will plead for anything to believe in.

Education is freedom

Education is the instrument that differentiates between the dead and living.

Serving two masters

Two natures battle in our hearts to
see which is the master,
either the storm cloud
or the disaster.

An eternal conflict

As the fall in heaven so on earth,
the war within so without. Thoughts
and emotions will go the way they
are diverted. And free will was the
downfall of man, for he chose to
call condemnation forth and has
created the universe exactly
as it is. This most difficult game
and the imponderable questions
to life are the same.

I am

I am the fragile flower and the infinite star in the cosmos that never fades. I have stumbled and blundered fighting life's brutal battles. Surrounded by snakes like scavengers, still I triumph over the trials and troubles, and snakes with poison fangs and rattles. I'll never die forever, I'll be back baptised in eternal fire, full of hope and desire.

Rebirth

At dawn, rise as
a different man
than the one you
fell asleep as. And
behold today's
death is tomorrow's
resurrection.

Caterpillar and butterfly

The caterpillar and butterfly
differ in shape and colour, but
in origin, both life forms began
in a cocoon, and are one and
the same inside.

The measure of a man

If the dry land is fashioned from dust and the sea
from droplets of water, then is
not man much greater than this?
Consider a tree, it is acknowledged
by its roots that flourish in the earth, and
when it bears and nourishes good
fruit. Therefore measure a man by
his actions, for words are an empty
shell without deeds.

The scent after the crush

The burden of the past is
the lesson for the present.
Do not let tomorrow's uncertainty
steal from today's joy and possibility.
A chick hatches through an internal
force out of the eggshell to existence.
A flower giveth a pleasant scent after
being crushed; therefore, life
begins when one is broken from within.
Your confidence shatters your action, so
forgive before the rooster crows.
And behold, be a reflection of what you
want others to do unto you.

The gate of life

The gate of life is heavy, and it is difficult to sweep the doorsteps. Thieves seek to climb in at the window, but ye who knock will find the door swings wide open.

The emotion of God

When a man hurts a woman, he is not only crushing his own heart, but vexes God, for he fashioned in woman His love and strength, therefore what you do to her you do to God too.

Clock of life

Life is like a clock where death knocks once, and man has no power to delay nor extend the hour.

Forgiveness

Forgiveness is like an umbrella, it may not ease the storm, but it can let us stand in the rain.

The church

The church is not a museum for the wealthy, but it is a resting home for the poor and a hospital for the wounded.

Wise as a serpent

Be wise as a serpent and harmless
as the lamb among a pack
of wolves. Choose your
friends astutely, for
a lion cannot befriend
a deer.

The youth of today

The young hearts with an old soul,
hungry and naïve, they
swallow their instincts and
accept anything the world
offers them to eat.

Nowhere to rest

The weary have a place to nest, but the greater entity has a swarm of wasps in his head and no pillow to rest.

The voice of the enemy

The media is the voice of the enemy that shatters laws and betrays the deepest trust to silence those who value the conscience.

The stony path

Consider the broad and narrow way; one is a choice and the other is your fate. The road with an eternal view is only chosen by few, for it is a stony path and a difficult one to follow if you enter this door. Although both routes have an end, their consequences are different, as one holds life and the other destruction.

Peace is at hand

Even though in combat,
peace is at hand.
It exists deep within,
but when it is sought
outside, it is like the
heat that wilts the
flower.

Abomination

Whoever slaughters a man, it is like the
killing of God, since we all are his canvas.

Death does not exist

Death does not exist
when life possesses faith.

Give in to love

Men are slaves of fear and their nature is to destroy that which they value the most. Therefore, unless man submits to love and denies himself, he will not accept the existence of the spirit of light in him.

Life's greatest treasure

Our desire for possessions develops the instrument for destruction. But life's greatest pleasure exists in the simplest things.

Labour with love

Let us labour with love, for it was once the lace that tied all shoes together.

Deceitful cats

Pay attention to the mission,
for the flock of cats have risen
just to skim the cream from the
people's milk.

Man's deepest fear

Man's deepest fear is that the
promise of eternal existence
could be life's greatest lie.

The divine state

Knowledge is a divine state and men cannot experience that which they do not know. That which moved energy to create matter was a pure thought, and time was formed when the elements sprang forth in the realm of the relative, not the absolute.

The sower

Be the sower of time
and strive without end.

The system

Conform or be cursed, the system is corrupted
online as it is in reality.
It is designed to enslave the masses, punish the innocent
and protect the convicts.

The voice within

The courts of justice may fail to punish the guilty,
but there is no more powerful judge than the conscience,
thus it is better to be accused by men than to
act against the voice within.

The shadow of death

Seeds will rot, not grow,
And become marionettes.
Lives will be on a chip, existence fed
through a wire. The warmth of the sun
will not exist, neither will the moon shine.
Hearts will be paved with venom,
Wolves will dwell in the head,
War shall entwine the east with the west,
the north with the south.
The days will not carry pleasure,
nor will the night bring rest.
Heaven will close its gate
and earth open its mouth,
And the cup of suffering will be
poured and the sword of death drawn.

Proverbs 1

Poverty attracts desire and absence amplifies it. Those who hunger and thirst will ask, emptiness forces us to seek and silence makes us knock.

Proverbs 2

A guilty conscience fears all. Therefore be master of your will and life will spring with riches.

Proverbs 3

Pain is the price of consciousness, but be like a child and you will be resilient.

Proverbs 4

The road to life is paved with thorns and the path to glory is filled with thistle.

Proverbs 5

When the rope ends, it is the worth of the line that ties birth and death that counts.

Proverbs 6

Know suffering to hold peace, the valley of love is forbearance. Be clothed with humility, to forgive and free the chaos and doubts that burden your mind.

Proverbs 7

Be a servant first, then will you be a master

Proverbs 8

Darkness begets light, in light there is no darkness, Life brings death, and in death is life.

Proverbs 9

Patience is a symbol of inner peace.

Proverbs 10

Darkness is seldom eternal, but he that endures it shall overcome it and witness the break of dawn.

Proverbs 11

Pain plants lessons to grow, but pride prevents learning, And he that blossoms in faith will have joy radiating like the fragrance from a flower.

Proverbs 12

Love is naked and gives. Fear is clothed and grasps.

Proverbs 13

That which limits us is our knowingness, but the trouble is, in the blink of an eye, everything that you hold dear will end.

Proverbs 14

That which you fear most will possess you, but know that the mind will always be disabled by the shadow of doubts. The key is to conquer these clouds of thoughts and make the choice before convincing yourself you need more time.

When the sun sets

Centuries have come and gone. Humanity has stared at sunrises, but refused to ask where ye shall be when the day is done. Will mankind rise to see the golden morning glow in the land that knows no sunset, or fall unto the darkness of night where heaven's light is out of sight?

Haile Tesfaye

www.ingramcontent.com/pod-product-compliance
Lightning Source LLC
Chambersburg PA
CBHW042338150426
43195CB00001B/28